MALCOLM X

Biography.

MALCOLM X

Michael Benson

Lerner Publications Company
Minneapolis

*This book is lovingly dedicated
to my Aunt Bettie*

A&E and **BIOGRAPHY** are trademarks of the A&E Television Networks, registered in the United States and other countries.

Some of the people profiled in this series have also been featured in A&E's acclaimed BIOGRAPHY series, which is available on videocassette from A&E Home Video. Call 1-800-423-1212 to order.

Lerner Publications Company
A division of Lerner Publishing Group
241 First Avenue North
Minneapolis, MN 55401 U.S.A.

Website address: www.lernerbooks.com

Library of Congress Cataloging-in-Publication Data

Benson, Michael.
    Malcolm X / by Michael Benson.
        p. cm.
    Includes bibliographical references and index.
    ISBN: 0–8225–5025–3 (lib. bdg. : alk. paper)
    1. X, Malcolm, 1925–1965. 2. Black Muslims—Biography—Juvenile
literature. 3. Afro-Americans—Biography—Juvenile literature.
    [1. X, Malcolm, 1925–1965. 2. Black Muslims—Biography.
    3. Afro-Americans—Biography.] I. Title.
    BP223.Z8 L5719 2002
    320.54'092—dc21   00–011640

Manufactured in the United States of America
1 2 3 4 5 6 – JR – 07 06 05 04 03 02

CONTENTS

1 Terror in the Night 7

2 Hustling 19

3 Prison Conversion 29

4 Minister 37

5 Nature Fails 51

6 True Islam 67

7 World Leader 75

8 Threats and Danger 83

9 Malcolm's Legacy 97

Sources 106

Selected Bibliography 108

Index 109

During the early years of Malcolm X's life, segregation in public places, such as buses, was common.

Chapter **ONE**

TERROR IN THE NIGHT

MALCOLM **X** WAS BORN INTO A DIFFERENT TIME, a time when black men and women were supposed to smilingly and quietly accept their role as second-class citizens. It was a time when black people, who were politely called Negroes in those days, were expected to sit at the back of the bus. They were not allowed to use "whites-only" drinking fountains, restaurants, or rest rooms in the South. Worst of all, black people in America were not supposed to have any ambition. They had no choice but to work for little money—the alternative was to starve.

Most white people encouraged the system because they saved a lot of money in wages they did not have to pay. Besides, they believed they were behaving according to human nature. People, no matter what color they are, do not give up the power they have—not without a fight.

EARLY YEARS

Malcolm Little was born on May 19, 1925, in Omaha, Nebraska, the son of Louise and Earl Little. Earl was a tall, dark-skinned Baptist minister from Reynolds, Georgia. He was not the sort of man to quietly accept his role as a second-class citizen. On the contrary, Earl Little was a human rights activist. He told anyone who would listen that black people should remove themselves from white society. He believed that blacks could not win in this system.

When Earl wasn't doing odd jobs to pay his family's bills, he worked for Marcus Garvey, a political activist who believed that African Americans should return to the continent of their origin—that is, Africa.

Louise, Earl's second wife, was born in Grenada in the British West Indies. She was half white and half black. Louise was a well-educated woman, but her education did not do her much good in the United States, where black women could find work only in unskilled jobs such as housekeeping.

Malcolm was the fourth of eight children. The oldest was Wilfred. Then came Hilda, Philbert, and Malcolm. Malcolm was followed by Reginald, Yvonne, Wesley, and Robert. Malcolm also had three older half-siblings

Marcus Garvey, born in 1887 in Jamaica, formed the Universal Negro Improvement Association (UNIA) and later the African Communities League. His goal was to foster unity among black people everywhere and to promote black pride.

from his father's first marriage. These siblings, Ella, Earl, and Mary, lived in Boston.

Malcolm was the lightest child in the family, taking after his mother more than his father. Malcolm's hair and skin were sandy brown, while his brothers and sisters had darker coloring.

THE HAZARDS OF BEING BLACK

Although many decades had passed since slaves were freed at the end of the Civil War, living conditions for black people had not improved greatly. Only the most menial and low-paying jobs, such as janitor and dishwasher, were available for black people. Even their freedom of movement was restricted.

When Malcolm was a little boy, it was illegal in many towns for a black person to be out in public (that is, in the white section of town) after dark.

In the southern states, the races were kept apart, or segregated, by laws that required separate public facilities for whites and blacks. Drinking fountains, train and bus stations, rest rooms, and theaters were designated "White" or "Colored." Black kids could not attend school with white kids, and they were kept out of libraries, parks, and pools. While white kids attended schools in nice brick buildings, black children went to school in rundown, overcrowded shacks. Whites in the South devised ways of keeping black people from voting by making them pay to vote or

Drinking fountains and other public facilities in the South were segregated by color in the 1920s and 1930s, when Malcolm was a young boy.

pass a reading test. The system of segregation affected almost every aspect of life in the South.

In the northern states, while segregation was not a legal institution as it was in the South, black people were still treated unfairly. Even as many black families migrated north in search of better opportunities, they discovered that good jobs and housing were hard to come by. In 1917 ten thousand black people had marched on Fifth Avenue in New York City to protest the lack of good jobs and racial discrimination.

Black people who spoke out about their lack of civil rights were considered "troublemakers" by white people—and by some black people, too. Some blacks worried that when white people came after the troublemakers, all black people were going to end up getting hurt.

The danger was real. White racist groups such as the Ku Klux Klan (KKK) terrorized black people, especially those who tried to fight the injustices of racial segregation and discrimination. Klansmen were known for the white hoods they wore and the burning crosses they utilized as threats. Many blacks were lynched (killed, often by hanging) by the Klan and other white mobs.

The Garvey organization for which Malcolm's father and mother worked was called the Universal Negro Improvement Association (UNIA). As long as the Littles were active in UNIA, the family was in danger. One night just before Malcolm was born, a group of white-hooded Klansmen on horseback rode in around the

The Ku Klux Klan, shown here around a burning cross in Wrightsville, Georgia, terrorized the Little family and other black citizens.

Littles' house, breaking every window with the butts of their shotguns before riding off. After a number of these threats, the Littles decided to leave Nebraska.

Fleeing the KKK, the Littles moved to Milwaukee, Wisconsin. The family did not stay there long, however. They moved to Albion, Michigan, which had been an Underground Railroad "station" during the Civil War. Still looking for better circumstances, Earl next moved the family to Lansing, Michigan. Malcolm was four years old.

For a time, Malcolm's home life was loving, though chaotic. His mother was always working. His parents were often arguing. But the children were happy. Malcolm was a smart, spirited child who learned early on that he stood a better chance of getting what he wanted by "making a fuss" than by being nice and quiet. He was especially pleased when his father took him in a big black touring car to UNIA meetings, where Earl would speak. Malcolm loved watching his father speak and preach.

THE EARLY CIVIL RIGHTS MOVEMENT

Ever since the time of slavery, African Americans have fought for equal rights as U.S. citizens. One of the oldest civil rights organizations in the country, the National Association for the Advancement of Colored People (NAACP), was established in 1909 in response to the 1908 lynching of two black men in Springfield, Illinois. The NAACP worked to eliminate racial discrimination and segregation through peaceful and legal means, such as court challenges to racist laws. In its early years, the group focused on anti-lynching bills and measures to end tactics used by white people to keep black people from voting.

Demands for civil rights reached a new peak during World War II. More than one million black soldiers joined the fight against Adolf Hitler's Nazi regime, even as they were still treated as second-class citizens back home. Blacks protested the army's policy of segregation and worked to end discrimination in the defense industry, which hired few black workers. Among 100,000 aircraft workers in 1940, only 240 were black.

In 1942 James Farmer founded the Congress of Racial Equality (CORE). He wanted to fight discrimination using "passive resistance," techniques that Indian leader Mohandas Gandhi used against the British colonizers in India. CORE pioneered two techniques that were used throughout the Civil Rights movement—the sit-in, in which black people refused to leave a place designated for whites, and the "freedom ride," in which black people challenged segregated seating on buses.

During the war, NAACP membership soared. In the late 1940s and early 1950s, lawyers for the organization argued a series of important segregation cases before the Supreme Court. These cases resulted in a landmark decision declaring that separate schools for blacks were unconstitutional. These developments set the stage for the Civil Rights movement of the 1950s and 1960s.

The family raised chickens and had a big garden. Malcolm had his own small plot to tend in the garden. He loved taking care of it and was particularly proud of the peas he grew. "I would pull out the grass in my garden by hand when the first little blades came up," he recalled. "I would patrol the rows on my hands and knees for any worms and bugs, and I would kill and bury them. And sometimes when I had everything straight and clean for my things to grow, I would lie down on my back between two rows, and I would gaze up in the blue sky at the clouds moving and think all kinds of things."

In 1929 Earl bought a house in a white section of Lansing. Neighbors were appalled that a black family had moved onto the block. They immediately claimed that by law, the house had to be sold to white people. When the Littles refused to move, a mob surrounded the house in the middle of the night. Malcolm's mother came to the door. The mob demanded to see Earl. She told them he was out of town.

The mob then set fire to the house. Malcolm's first vivid memory from his childhood was of standing in the backyard in his underwear in the middle of the night as his home burned. "The white police and firemen came and stood around watching as the house burned down to the ground," he wrote later.

Earl built his family a new home, but the Littles' problems were far from over. The white racists of Lansing were not through with them. In 1931, when

Malcolm was six years old, some men came to the house with the news that Earl Little was dead. He had been beaten and laid across the railroad tracks. He wasn't found until after a trolley car had run over him.

To ensure that his family would have money to live on in case something happened to him, Earl had bought a large insurance policy. But when he died, the money did not come from the insurance company. After an "investigation," the company claimed that Earl had bashed in his own head and dragged himself across the railroad tracks. The company refused to pay off his policy, saying that Earl had committed suicide.

A SCATTERED FAMILY

At first Louise was able to land a good job because she was light-skinned enough to be mistaken for a white woman. But when her employer saw Louise's children and realized that she was black, she was fired. Louise was very frustrated because she could not use the good education she had received in Grenada.

She did her best to keep the family together, but eventually the stress became too much for her. Malcolm began to notice a difference in his mother. Sometimes she seemed unaware of her surroundings. She began to talk to herself. At times it was as if she didn't know that Malcolm and his brothers and sisters were in the room with her. It seemed like she cried all the time.

Welfare workers began coming to the house and asking the children questions. Louise Little became increasingly hostile to the welfare people. She knew what they were up to—they were trying to break up her family. In 1937 Louise was committed to a mental institution. Her children became "wards of the state"—orphans. They were split up and sent to foster homes. Malcolm lived with a friendly neighboring family, the Gohannases. Despite their separation, the Little children continued to get together whenever they could.

Following his father's death, Malcolm got into trouble more and more. He was expelled from sixth grade after he put a tack on his teacher's seat. That prank earned him a stint in a detention home in Mason, Michigan. The following fall, he started seventh grade in a new school, where he was the only black student. Malcolm did well in his classes and was popular with the other students. He was even elected class president. Malcolm later said that the white people didn't really see him as a human being but as a "mascot" or pet. He felt that their acceptance of him was not genuine.

While Malcolm was attending junior high school, he met his half-sister Ella for the first time when she came from Boston to visit her siblings in Michigan. Ella was a distinguished and intelligent twenty-four-year-old. She had worked hard, saved money, and invested in property that had increased in value. She had helped other family members move to Boston and get established. Malcolm was very impressed with her.

"She was the first really proud black woman I had ever seen in my life," he wrote. "She was plainly proud of her very dark skin. This was unheard of among Negroes in those days, especially in Lansing. . . . The way she sat, moved, talked, did everything, bespoke somebody who did and got exactly what she wanted."

A turning point in Malcolm's life came later that year. One day at school, Malcolm's English teacher, Mr. Ostrowski, asked him what he wanted to be when he grew up. Malcolm replied that he was thinking of becoming a lawyer. His teacher said, "Malcolm, one of life's first needs is for us to be realistic. Don't misunderstand me, now. We all here like you, you know that. But you've got to be realistic about being a nigger. A lawyer—that's no realistic goal for a nigger. You need to think of something you *can* be. . . . Why don't you plan on carpentry?"

Malcolm was devastated when he heard this. There no longer seemed to be any point in dreaming. He realized that it was useless for a black man to have any ambitions in a society controlled by whites. Soon afterward, Malcolm began to write to his sister Ella, telling her how much he would like to come to Boston. Ella agreed and arranged for legal custody of Malcolm. In 1940, at age fifteen, Malcolm ended his formal education and headed for Boston to see what he could learn on his own.

Malcolm X with his half-sister Ella outside of her home in
Boston. Hungry for freedom, fifteen-year-old Malcolm moved
there from Lansing, Michigan, in 1940.

Chapter **TWO**

HUSTLING

FIFTEEN-YEAR-OLD **MALCOLM WAS OVER SIX FEET** tall and slender. Looking older and more mature than he was, he told Ella that he wanted to get a job. She said fine, but not right away. First he should get to know the city, especially Roxbury, a black neighborhood in Boston. Later, she said, she would help him get a job.

Ella hoped that Malcolm would use this period of freedom to mix with the high society of Roxbury, who lived in the section known as the Hill. But that is not what Malcolm did. Instead, he immediately familiarized himself with Roxbury's seedy bars and pool halls. At one of the pool halls, Malcolm met a man named Shorty Jarvis, who was racking billiard balls. Shorty was also from Lansing. He could see that Malcolm was still a little wet behind the ears—inexperienced in the ways of the street—so he showed him the ropes.

When Ella got Malcolm the job she'd promised, it turned out to be shining shoes at the Roseland Ballroom, a dance hall in Boston. The finest bands in the world, black and white, played at the Roseland. Shorty taught Malcolm some tricks of the shoeshine trade, ways to make the white men give bigger tips. Shorty told Malcolm to "Tom a little"—that is, to act like an Uncle Tom, a meek black man who behaves like a servant in front of white people. So Malcolm kept his head bowed as he snapped his buff rag.

Being a humble shoeshine boy did not fit Malcolm's style, however. He quickly learned that he could make a lot more money selling marijuana to Roseland's customers. Whether he was shining shoes or dealing drugs, Malcolm got to meet some of the greatest musicians of his day at Roseland, including Count Basie, Lionel Hampton, and Duke Ellington.

When he went out on the town, Malcolm dressed in a sharp-looking zoot suit. Zoot suits had wide shoulders and baggy trousers. Malcolm's suit (he had just one at first) was blue. He wore a matching wide-brimmed hat with a feather in it.

Shorty used lye to "conk," or straighten, Malcolm's hair in the style of the time. The word *conk* came from Congolene, one of the brand names for the

Fifteen-year-old Malcolm poses in his zoot suit, circa 1940.

chemical solution used to straighten black people's hair. Most people, however, like Malcolm and Shorty, used a homemade concoction of lye and potatoes instead of the more expensive Congolene.

"This was my first really big step toward self-degradation," Malcolm later wrote. "I endured all of that pain, literally burning my flesh to have it look like a white man's hair."

But Malcolm wasn't thinking in those terms when he had his hair straightened. He was thinking about dancing.

"Malcolm was like a Romeo," remembered Shorty Jarvis. "All the girls were after him."

Malcolm liked to dance with the ladies at the ballroom. "I just about went wild...," he said. "I was whirling girls so fast their skirts were snapping."

THE FAST LIFE

Malcolm soon quit his job at the Roseland and went to work as a soda fountain clerk in a shop near Ella's house, in the fashionable part of Roxbury. There he met a girl his age named Laura. She was just the sort of girl Ella wanted Malcolm to meet. Laura was interested in education, and she told Malcolm that it wasn't too late for him. If he went back to school, he could become a lawyer, just like he had dreamed.

No matter what Malcolm's teacher in Michigan had said, Laura explained, a black man could become a lawyer in America. It might not be as easy as it would be for a white person, but it could be done. But Malcolm was too caught up in his street ways to hear what she was saying.

One night soon after they began dating, Malcolm took Laura to a dance at the Roseland Ballroom. While there, he met a woman named Sophia. In the autobiography that Malcolm wrote later, he didn't mention Sophia's last name or her age, but he made it clear that she was older, experienced, and wild. Malcolm abruptly took Laura home and returned to meet Sophia, who was white. According to Malcolm, Laura was so humiliated by the experience that her life fell apart.

Malcolm wasn't interested in a serious relationship or in anything that promised long-term benefits. Like many young men his age, he was more interested in the kicks he could get right away. It was that kind of thinking that increasingly led him into a life of crime.

Malcolm had heard that, when it came to wild fun and excitement, Harlem was the place to be. Harlem, a neighborhood in the northern part of New York City, was the center of black culture, a place where the hottest music was played and the hippest people hung out. Malcolm got his chance to go there in December 1941, the same month that Japanese forces bombed Pearl Harbor, Hawaii. This event marked the beginning of the United States' involvement in World War II.

That month, Malcolm landed a job working for the Yankee Clipper train, which traveled between Boston and New York. He was a kitchen helper, assigned to wash dishes, take out the garbage, sell sandwiches to passengers, and clean up after the chef.

As soon as Malcolm got a taste of the pulsing rhythms of Harlem, he knew that this was where he wanted to be. He was only sixteen, but he moved out of his sister's house and into a boardinghouse in Harlem.

DETROIT RED

Away from Ella, Malcolm quickly fell into bad habits. He not only continued to sell marijuana, but he also smoked a lot of it himself. He began using cocaine as well. The drugs made him feel as if he were in control of himself, but in reality he was not. Because of the cocaine, Malcolm was often aggressive and obnoxious while carrying out his duties on the train. The customers complained, and it wasn't long before Malcolm was fired.

His next job was working at a Harlem restaurant called Small's Paradise, a hangout for Harlem criminal types. Among the colorfully named people that Malcolm met at Small's Paradise were West Indian Archie, Sammy the Pimp, Dollarbill, and Fewclothes. Malcolm picked up a nickname of his own during this time. Because of his reddish skin and hair and his Michigan upbringing, his street name became Detroit Red.

Besides working as a waiter, Malcolm made extra money as a "steerer." If someone, usually a white man, came to Harlem looking for drugs or prostitutes, Malcolm's job was to steer the person to the right place.

"He was a beautiful con man," Shorty Jarvis said of his friend. "He was a thinker."

Malcolm's crimes kept getting worse. Soon he and his buddies were engaging in armed robberies. It never occurred to Malcolm to feel guilty about his criminal behavior. He believed that in a white-controlled society a black man didn't stand a chance of making an honest living. His only option was "hustling," as people on the streets called it.

"Everybody in Harlem needed some kind of hustle to survive," he said.

Malcolm ended up losing his job at Small's. He "steered" a man to a prostitute and the man turned out to be a police informant.

Several times during these months, Malcolm almost lost his life due to his risky lifestyle. He never went anywhere without packing several handguns. When an argument broke out with another hustler, neither side was going to back down, and the guns often came out. At least once, Malcolm was roughed up by Harlem gangsters who thought he had ripped them off in a drug deal. Life on the streets was becoming increasingly dangerous, but Malcolm did nothing to change his ways because he saw no alternative.

After losing his job at Small's, Malcolm did not get another real job. Instead, taking the advice of Sammy the Pimp, he became a full-time criminal.

HARD TIMES IN HARLEM

Malcolm turned eighteen in May 1943. With World War II still raging, he was ordered to appear before the draft board. But Malcolm had no intention of being inducted (enrolled) into the army to fight what he considered the white man's war. He came up with a plan—he would act crazy during the physical examination required for the induction process.

According to Malcolm's version of the story, he wore his most outrageous zoot suit to the draft interview, and he told the psychiatrists who interviewed him that he couldn't wait to get a gun and start shooting white folks. That did it. Malcolm was declared 4-F, or ineligible for the military.

At the time, racial tensions in Harlem were heating up. Although the war helped the United States move out of the crippling economic depression that had gripped the country since 1929, the economic situation in Harlem and other black communities was worse than ever.

A young Harlem politician named Adam Clayton Powell Jr. led protests against the lack of jobs and housing for black people. These protests raised African Americans' awareness of the problems. The building anger in Harlem exploded one night in August 1943, when a black soldier was shot to death by a white New York City police officer in a Harlem hotel. Riots broke out. Five people were killed and more than four hundred were injured.

The riots also killed what was left of the Harlem economy. Because of the racial tension, white people stopped going to Harlem and spending money at the music clubs. They no longer felt safe in Harlem. The community became poorer than ever.

For a time, Malcolm made money running numbers—taking part in the illegal lottery held by gangsters in Harlem. Things got even worse for him when he was

A mounted police officer patrols a Harlem street after the night of riots on August 2, 1943. The disturbances began after a black soldier was shot and killed by a white police officer.

accused of cheating in a card game. West Indian Archie swore that he would kill Malcolm. Word got out that Malcolm was in big trouble. The news even made it up to Boston.

Malcolm was moving from shadow to shadow one night when a car pulled up to the curb. It was Malcolm's old friend Shorty Jarvis. Shorty told him to get in, and he took him to Boston, an act that probably saved Malcolm's life.

A police mug shot of Malcolm X after his arrest in 1945

Chapter **THREE**

PRISON CONVERSION

MALCOLM HAD MADE A LOT OF MONEY IN New York, but when he arrived in Boston in 1945, he was broke. Most of his money had gone to pay for his drug habit. Malcolm was spending twenty dollars a day for cocaine and five dollars a day for marijuana.

In Boston, Malcolm and his girlfriend Sophia, whom he'd continued to see over the years, set up a burglary business along with Shorty and his girlfriend. Since the women were white, they were sent out in advance to check out houses to see if anyone was home. They would come back and tell Malcolm and Shorty, who would then go out and rob the unoccupied homes. They sold the goods to pawnshops.

In one house, Malcolm stole a watch that needed repair. The owner of the watch reported that it had been stolen and told the police that it was broken. When Malcolm took the watch to a repair shop, the police were casing the place, and Malcolm was arrested. He and Shorty were convicted of burglary, and Malcolm was sentenced to ten years in prison. That was more time than most burglars got for a first offense.

"We were given that time because we associated with white girls," said Shorty, whose sentence was even longer than Malcolm's.

Malcolm and Shorty entered Charlestown State Prison in Boston in February 1946. Malcolm was twenty years old. Shorty described the hardships they had to endure in prison: "The cell was six by twelve feet. You got a hard cot, a bucket of water, and a bucket for defecation. No running water. Unsanitary. Filthy!"

THE BLACK MUSLIMS

While in prison, Malcolm heard about the Nation of Islam, a fringe religious sect headed by a man named Elijah Muhammad. Malcolm's brothers Philbert and Reginald visited him and urged him to join the Nation. The group, which was based on the world religion of Islam, worshiped Allah as God.

The Black Muslims, as they were informally known, believed strongly in two things: 1) White people were, by nature, corrupt. They were the source of all evil and were therefore considered devils; 2) Blacks, as Allah's chosen people, were destined to rise above the white devils. These statements may seem extreme, but to Malcolm—who had seen his father murdered by white people and his mother's subsequent mental collapse—they made a lot of sense.

The teachings of Elijah Muhammad also reminded Malcolm of the ideas that his father and Marcus Garvey had promoted. Malcolm no doubt saw Elijah Muhammad as a father figure. After all, Elijah and Earl Little had been born only seventy miles apart in rural Georgia, and both men embraced similar philosophies, concentrating on black pride and brotherhood. And, like Earl Little, Elijah had moved to Michigan in hopes of finding freedom and opportunity.

Elijah Muhammad, seated, and the Nation of Islam had a profound influence on Malcolm. Also pictured are, left to right, bodyguards Herbert Muhammad (Elijah's son), John Ali and James Shab.

What Malcolm did not know was that the teachings of the Nation of Islam differed drastically from those of traditional Islam. The Islamic religion, as practiced in the Middle East and elsewhere, teaches that all people are brothers and sisters, regardless of race. The Nation of Islam, on the other hand, taught that the black race was God's favorite and that white people were evil disciples of the devil. Unlike traditional Muslims, or followers of Islam, members of the Nation of Islam recognized Elijah Muhammad as a prophet, a man to be worshiped as God.

In 1948 Malcolm was transferred to Norfolk Prison Colony, also in Massachusetts. This prison was nicer than the previous one—at least the toilets flushed. In late 1949, Malcolm began to correspond with Elijah Muhammad, and he declared himself a Muslim. Malcolm adopted the habits of the Black Muslims, who believed in cleanliness of the body, mind, and spirit. Members did not drink, smoke, or eat pork. They did not have sex outside of marriage.

WORD POWER

The prison had a surprisingly large library, a gift left in someone's will. To educate himself and to improve his penmanship, Malcolm copied one page from the dictionary into a notebook each day. He also read an encyclopedia and many other books. Malcolm read the Bible, H. G. Wells's *Outline of History*, books about genetics, and the classic antislavery novel *Uncle Tom's*

In 1947 members of the Nation of Islam gathered in prayer to celebrate Ramadan, a thirty-day fast observed in the ninth month of the Islamic year.

Cabin. When Malcolm started his self-improvement program, he had a working vocabulary of less than two hundred words and his handwriting was so poor that he could not write in a straight line. By 1950 he had tremendously increased his vocabulary and knowledge of world events and history.

With his newfound word power, Malcolm began a letter-writing campaign, working on behalf of the Nation of Islam. In addition to daily letters to his brothers Philbert and Reginald, his sister Hilda, and Elijah Muhammad, Malcolm wrote to government officials demanding an end to racial injustice. He also sent letters to many of his old criminal friends, letting them know that he had changed his ways and inviting them to join the Nation of Islam.

Even after the 10:00 P.M. "lights out" in the prison, Malcolm continued to read, studying philosophy, science, and religion until the early morning hours. He used the light that came into his cell from the hallway. When a guard passed, Malcolm moved to his bunk and pretended to be asleep. Later, he blamed these many hours of reading in low light for his need to wear glasses.

Malcolm organized discussion groups in prison for those interested in learning about the Black Muslims. He mixed stories of past African civilizations with tales

ELIJAH MUHAMMAD

Elijah Muhammad was born Elijah Poole around October 7, 1897, in a rural part of Georgia known as Sandersville. The exact date of his birth is uncertain because of poor record keeping in the area at that time. Elijah was one of twelve children of William and Marie Poole. His father was a minister. In 1919 Elijah married a woman named Clara Evans. The couple eventually had eight children. At the time of his marriage, Elijah worked for both the railroad and a brick company. But in April 1923, he took his family north to Detroit, Michigan, where he got a job working on an automobile assembly line.

In 1930 Elijah met the founder of the Nation of Islam (then known as the Temple of Islam), Wallace D. Fard, who preached that it was time for black people to return to Islam, the religion of their ancestors. When Elijah met him, Fard was selling silk products door to door, but he said he was a prophet who came from Africa to help American blacks understand their heritage. The black race, according to Fard, was the superior "original race," and black Americans were Islam's lost sheep. His job was to herd the sheep and bring them back home.

According to Elijah's later teachings, he learned from Fard that in the early days of the world, black men were in charge.

of white oppression in modern times. Prisoners who knew him when he first arrived—as an angry young man they called "Satan"—were amazed at the change that had come over him after his religious conversion. Still angry, Malcolm was now extremely focused, and he hoped to use his anger to improve the world.

Black scientists, Fard claimed, created the seas and the mountains. They were in contact with nine-foot-tall men from Mars who caused the moon to blast into orbit around the Earth from its previous place beneath the Pacific Ocean.

Elijah became Fard's chief aide and devoted disciple. Fard gave Elijah his Muslim name, Muhammad. In 1934 Elijah was arrested for encouraging Black Muslim parents to send their children to Muslim schools, which were not considered legitimate schools by the Michigan State Board of Education. Elijah did not serve jail time, but his schools were closed down. In response, Elijah, along with Fard, moved to Chicago, Illinois.

Fard disappeared on February 26, 1934, and to this day no one knows what happened to him. After his disappearance, Elijah took control of the Nation of Islam.

The next year, Elijah moved to Washington, D.C., after hearing rumors of death threats against him. In 1942, during World War II, Elijah was arrested, along with many other Black Muslims, for draft evasion. Elijah was imprisoned, even though he was forty-five years old—too old to be drafted. He was not released from prison until World War II ended, in 1945.

In the years following the war, the Nation of Islam went on a membership drive, preaching the message of black power to people in ghettos and prisons. This is when Malcolm X was brought into the fold.

Malcolm X, pictured in the early 1960s, wore closely cropped hair and neat suits.

Chapter **FOUR**

MINISTER

MALCOLM WAS RELEASED FROM PRISON ON PAROLE in August 1952. (Under the parole system, a prisoner is released before his full sentence is up. He remains free as long as he stays out of trouble and stays in touch with a parole officer.) A free man, Malcolm immediately went to Detroit to live with his brother Wilfred, who managed a furniture store. Wilfred gave Malcolm a job there as a salesperson.

Malcolm no longer wore his hair straightened, but kept it natural and close-cropped in the style of Black Muslim men, who looked sharp in their black suits, white shirts, and slender black ties. Malcolm replaced his prison eyeglasses with a more attractive pair.

Malcolm attended meetings at Nation of Islam Temple Number One in Detroit with Wilfred and his family. (In the Islamic religion, worship takes place in a temple or mosque. The Nation of Islam first established temples that were numbered, such as Temple Number One in Detroit and Temple Number Two in Chicago. In later years, the temples were known as mosques.) Because of his good speaking skills, Malcolm was given the task of recruiting new members. He also continued to read many books and study the teachings of Elijah Muhammad.

ELIJAH

Malcolm finally got to meet the Honorable Elijah Muhammad himself at a meeting in Detroit on Labor Day 1952. Malcolm hadn't been so excited about anything since he was a child. During the meeting, Elijah Muhammad commended Malcolm for being so strong and for keeping up the Muslim traditions while he was in prison.

Then Elijah told Malcolm that it was easy to be good in prison. Now, with the temptations of the outside world before him, it remained to be seen how he would do. Elijah added that he was sure Malcolm was going to remain a faithful Black Muslim despite his freedom.

Malcolm openly worshiped Elijah. "I had more faith in Elijah Muhammad than I could ever have in any other man upon this earth," he said.

The Nation of Islam believed that a black man's last name was meaningless. During the period of slavery in the United States, black people usually didn't have a last name, since the names of their ancestors in Africa were long forgotten or ignored. When slaves became free, they usually took the name of their white slavemaster so that separated family members would have an easier time finding one another.

The Nation of Islam encouraged its members to unshackle themselves of their slave names. In place of that name, members used an X, which symbolized the unknown original African name. (The Black Muslims kept their first names, since these were given to them by their parents and not by white slavemasters.) When someone wanted to join the Nation of Islam, he or she had to make an application to Elijah Muhammad. When the application was approved, the applicant received his or her X. The new member was referred to as X until Elijah later gave the member a new, Islamic name.

To avoid having several members with the same name, the Xs were numbered. The first man named John who received his X from Elijah Muhammad became John X. The second man named John was John 2X, and so on. (Eventually people took an entirely new, Islamic name. Malcolm, for example, eventually took the name el-Hajj Malik el-Shabazz.) For Malcolm, taking the name X was the final step in separating himself from the person he had been before he began following the teachings of Elijah Muhammad.

A large crowd gathers at a Nation of Islam rally in Chicago, Illinois.

SPREADING THE WORD

Malcolm X proved to be very skilled at recruiting new members into the Nation. Although he was frustrated that he wasn't attracting new members at a faster pace, Malcolm was one of Elijah Muhammad's best recruiters from the start. His success helped move him into a new role. In the summer of 1953, Malcolm was named assistant minister at the temple in Detroit.

With the Korean War going on—a conflict that began in June 1950 between Communist North Korea and non-Communist South Korea, backed by the United States—Malcolm was once again called before the draft board. This time he did not act crazy to keep from being inducted into the military service. Instead, he refused to serve because of his religious beliefs—he was a conscientious objector. He told the board he believed that war was morally wrong and he therefore couldn't participate in one. The military men let him go.

In early 1954, Elijah sent Malcolm to Boston, where his sister Ella still lived, to establish a new temple. Malcolm caused quite a stir among his old cronies in Boston when they saw how he had changed. On the other hand, Malcolm was disturbed to see that his friends had not changed much at all—they had just gone farther down a bad road. They still lived a life of crime and were addicted to drugs.

When the Boston temple was set up and running smoothly, Elijah transferred Malcolm to Philadelphia. There he spent three months launching Temple Number Twelve.

With those successes under his belt, Elijah promoted Malcolm once again in the summer of 1954. In fact, he was given a dream assignment: minister of Temple Number Seven in Harlem. He went "fishing for souls" all over Harlem, and he was especially successful in the storefront Christian churches along the crowded avenues. Each week, more new faces appeared in the temple to hear Malcolm's fiery lectures. Malcolm gave great speeches. He preached the philosophy of Elijah Muhammad, but with the fire of Earl Little and a touch of the flamboyance of Marcus Garvey, the leader who had inspired Earl.

SISTER BETTY

In 1956 a new woman joined the Harlem temple. Sister Betty X, as Malcolm referred to her, had a fine mind and a strong spirit. Betty Sanders had been born in Detroit. She studied at the Tuskegee Institute, the Brooklyn State Hospital School of Nursing, and Jersey City State College. Malcolm sensed that Sister Betty could be his life's mate.

Malcolm arranged for Betty to meet Elijah Muhammad, who agreed that she was a fine woman. Malcolm took his time about it, but eventually he asked Betty to marry him. She said yes. Betty and Malcolm were married on January 14, 1958, by a justice of the peace in Lansing, Michigan.

Not long after Malcolm and Betty were married, Malcolm's sister Ella finally became part of the Nation of Islam. She had attended meetings for years but refused to join. Malcolm had figured she would never convert from Christianity. Her faith in Christianity had seemed so strong.

Sister Betty X

Another exciting milestone for the family came in November 1958. Malcolm and Betty's first child, a daughter they named Attallah, was born.

FIGHTING BACK

People in Harlem had certainly noticed the Nation of Islam, but the Black Muslims earned real respect in the community because of something that happened in April 1958. It began with the arrest and beating of a black man named Johnson Hinton. Hinton had seen the police beating another black man and had complained. Because he spoke out, the police turned on

Temple Number Seven members, led by Malcolm X, march to a New York Police Department station after the beating and arrest of an innocent black man.

Hinton and beat him also. Hinton, bleeding, was dragged to jail as if he had actually committed a crime.

When news of the police brutality reached Temple Number Seven, Malcolm formed a plan. He called temple members together, and they marched like an army to the police precinct where Hinton was being held. Malcolm entered the police station and demanded to see the prisoner. He explained that his men standing at attention outside would remain there until his demands were met.

In the meantime, outside the station, a crowd was gathering to see what all the fuss was about. Finally, Hinton was brought out to Malcolm. Malcolm demanded that Hinton be given medical attention. Only after Hinton was taken to the hospital did Malcolm tell his "soldiers" to leave.

Malcolm had stood up to the New York Police Department, and the officers had backed down. By the next day, everyone in Harlem knew about it. People viewed the Black Muslims with a new respect, and new recruits came in at a faster pace than ever.

Temple members were encouraged to start their own businesses and to live as much as possible outside the white man's economic system. The Nation of Islam was proud that many members owned their own businesses and, whenever possible, worked with black-owned companies.

Malcolm's message contrasted sharply with the goals and philosophy of the burgeoning, Christian-oriented Civil Rights movement. The movement got its start in December 1955, when a black woman named Rosa Parks was arrested in Montgomery, Alabama, because she refused to give up her seat on a bus to a white

Rosa Parks riding the bus in 1956

person. Her action motivated blacks in Montgomery to launch a boycott of the bus system. A local Baptist minister, Martin Luther King Jr., succeeded in transforming this local protest into a massive, nationwide resistance movement. After the boycott forced the Montgomery bus company to desegregate its facilities, picketing and boycotting spread rapidly to other towns and cities. From 1955 to 1960, civil rights activists used nonviolent means to integrate schools and other facilities, always facing bitter opposition by southern whites.

MARTIN LUTHER KING JR.

Martin Luther King Jr. was born on January 15, 1929, in Atlanta, Georgia, the son of a minister. Highly intelligent, Martin entered Morehouse College in Atlanta at age fifteen. He was ordained as a minister at nineteen, and by the time he was twenty-six years old, he had earned a doctorate degree.

During the late 1950s and early 1960s, Dr. King became an important figure in the Civil Rights movement. As president of the Montgomery (Alabama) Improvement Association, Martin organized a successful bus boycott in protest of laws that required black people to sit at the back of buses. After the successful boycott, King and other black ministers founded the Southern Christian Leadership Conference to fight for desegregation and civil rights in many other areas.

One of the great speakers of all time, Dr. King delivered his most famous speech in 1963. Following the March on Washington, D.C., which attracted hundreds of thousands of people of all colors to the nation's capital, Dr. King gave his "I Have a Dream" speech from the base of the Lincoln Memorial. He was named *Time* magazine's "Man of the Year" for 1963, and the next year he was awarded the Nobel Prize for Peace. Dr. King was assassinated on April 4, 1968, in Memphis, Tennessee.

Martin Luther King Jr. and Malcolm X tend to be lumped together in history books. Their philosophies were different, however. Dr. King organized freedom rides and protest marches to abolish segregation, and he favored integration between whites and blacks. Malcolm X and the Nation of Islam, on the other hand, believed that the races should live separately.

Dr. King followed a philosophy of nonviolence. Malcolm, however, believed that if a white man attacked a black man, the black man had the right to defend himself. Ultimately, Martin Luther King Jr. and Malcolm X understood that they shared the common goal of fighting oppression, despite their differing approaches.

Malcolm scorned these efforts and continued to call for black people to create their own society. Blacks could not afford to wait patiently for racial justice, he said. He opposed the goal of integration. "It is not integration that Negroes in America want, it is human dignity," he said. If Malcolm made one message clear, it was that black people were in charge of their own destiny.

Malcolm stressed the importance of knowing one's roots. In one speech, he said, "Royalty knows its ancestry. Royalty knows its history. That's what makes royalty royal. You can't have a king who can't trace his history back to his forefathers. The only way you can be a king is to be born a king. If you take away his history and he doesn't know who his forefathers were, what does he become? A peasant. A common, ordinary man."

In 1959 Malcolm began writing a column for the *Amsterdam News,* Harlem's community newspaper. Then, when Elijah Muhammad took over that column, Malcolm wrote for a time for the Los Angeles *Herald Dispatch,* a black weekly newspaper.

It was nice getting coverage of Nation of Islam ideas and events in big-city newspapers, but Malcolm thought it would be better if the Nation of Islam had its own paper. He formed *Muhammad Speaks,* a national newspaper that featured news stories and opinions from a Muslim point of view. The Nation was still not growing quickly enough for Malcolm.

New members were coming in dribbles, while he yearned for a flood.

Malcolm X holds up an issue of Muhammad Speaks *at a 1963 Black Muslim rally in New York City.*

Malcolm speaks at a rally in Washington, D.C., around 1960.

Chapter **FIVE**

NATURE FAILS

THE FLOOD OF ATTENTION THAT MALCOLM HOPED FOR came in late 1959, when CBS television's *The Mike Wallace Show* broadcast a documentary feature about the Nation of Islam. The show was called "The Hate That Hate Produced." It was produced by a black journalist named Louis Lomax, with the approval of Elijah Muhammad.

When the show aired, many people of all colors got their first glimpse of the charismatic young man with the unusual name of Malcolm X. The show included scenes shot in Nation of Islam temples in Washington, D.C., Chicago, and New York. Ministers, including Malcolm, were shown preaching about the brainwashing of black people by the white devils. The

documentary noted the Nation of Islam's economic independence from white people. Black Muslims only
dealt with white-owned companies when absolutely
necessary.

After the show, there was an uproar from both
whites and blacks who felt that the Nation of Islam
encouraged violence. Malcolm had never believed in
turning the other cheek. Instead, he insisted that
black people had the right to defend themselves if attacked by whites.

*Elijah Muhammad, right, introduces Malcolm X at a Chicago
rally on February 26, 1961.*

The television program produced another side effect. It opened the flood gates for new members. The Nation of Islam started holding national conventions, and Elijah Muhammad filled large arenas with his followers.

Malcolm X became an instant star—in fact, a superstar. The documentary captured his charismatic speaking style perfectly. Writer George Breitman described it this way: "His speaking style was unique—plain, direct as an arrow, devoid of flowery trimming. He used metaphors and figures of speech that were lean and simple, rooted in the ordinary experiences of his audiences. He knew what the masses think and how they feel, their strengths and weaknesses. He reached right into their minds and hearts without wasting a word; and he never tried to flatter them."

"Our forefathers weren't the Pilgrims," Malcolm would say. "We didn't land on Plymouth Rock. The Rock landed on us."

Even as Malcolm's phone was ringing off the hook with requests for interviews, the Federal Bureau of Investigation (FBI), fearful that the Nation of Islam was instigating violence and plotting revolution, was tapping his phone so they could listen in on his conversations. Malcolm suspected that his phone was tapped, but he couldn't prove it.

In September 1960, Malcolm gave the FBI even more to worry about when he met with the Cuban revolutionary leader Fidel Castro. Castro had turned

Cuba into a Communist nation and an enemy of the United States. (Other countries with Communist governments and economic systems included the Soviet Union and China.) When Castro came to New York, city officials prepared a hotel for him downtown. But Castro said he would rather stay in Harlem, and he wanted to meet Malcolm X.

After the meeting, Malcolm made it clear that the Nation of Islam could never form an alliance with Cuba because, as a Communist country, Cuba recognized no God. The FBI put Malcolm on its list of possible Communists anyway. Undercover FBI employees began to join the Nation of Islam to spy on him.

Over the next five years, the FBI became more and more convinced that Malcolm was a Communist. It was true that he increasingly blamed capitalism, the economic system of the United States, for the poor treatment that American blacks received. In a magazine interview, Malcolm said that in order for capitalism to thrive, it needed "blood to suck." That blood, he said, came from the most helpless people in society. But as these people gained power, capitalism would become weaker and weaker. "It's only a matter of time in my opinion before it will collapse completely," Malcolm said.

In December 1960, Betty gave birth to the couple's second daughter, Qubilah. In the meantime, Malcolm was spending more and more time working and less and less time with his family.

Malcolm X was very comfortable in front of the microphone and became the star of the Nation of Islam.

MALCOLM'S MESSAGE

As Malcolm's public statements became bolder and his power grew, the leader of the Nation of Islam was growing steadily weaker. Elijah Muhammad was not a young man, and he suffered from asthma. Sometimes his followers feared that he would not make it through a speech because of his coughing fits.

Eventually, Elijah's poor health forced him into semiretirement. He moved to Arizona, where the desert air was good for his lungs. Malcolm's role as national spokesman for the Nation of Islam became more important than ever. But Elijah's son, Wallace D.

Muhammad, and other top members of the Nation of Islam were jealous. They feared that Malcolm would take over the organization after Elijah was gone. Those close to Elijah kept Malcolm away from him as much as possible. They told Elijah lies about Malcolm so that Elijah would no longer trust his most successful minister.

Successful was hardly the word. Malcolm X had *become* the Nation of Islam. His speeches continued to draw new members, especially young black men and women from the urban ghettos. They agreed with Malcolm that the nonviolent protests of the Civil Rights movement were not producing results fast enough.

For the first time in four hundred years, Malcolm told audiences, blacks were learning the real truth—that white men had brainwashed black men and stolen their history and self-confidence. Malcolm taught that white men were evil because they oppressed and lynched black men.

"The white man has reveled as the rope snapped black men's necks. He has reveled around the lynching fire. . . . " Malcolm said. "The presence of 20 million black people here in America is proof that Uncle Sam is guilty of kidnapping—because we didn't come here voluntarily on the *Mayflower*. And 400 years of lynchings condemn Uncle Sam as a murderer."

But Malcolm's antiwhite stance offended many blacks. When a plane crashed in Atlanta, killing 120 white people, Malcolm referred to the event as "the good news."

One interviewer, hearing Malcolm preach that white men were evil, asked if Malcolm hated white people. Malcolm replied, "What I want to know is how the white man, with the blood of black people dripping off his fingers, can have the audacity to be asking black people do they hate him. That takes a lot of nerve."

In 1963 an adult magazine published an interview with Malcolm. The interview was conducted by Alex Haley, a black writer who later published the best-selling book *Roots*, which was made into a major television miniseries. Following the interview, Malcolm

Alex Haley, shown here with his best-selling book Roots, *interviewed Malcolm X in 1963 and later collaborated on Malcolm's autobiography.*

and Haley continued their collaboration, beginning work on Malcolm's autobiography.

In the magazine interview, Haley asked Malcolm what the Black Muslims' chief ambition was. Malcolm replied, "Freedom, justice and equality are our principal ambitions. And to faithfully serve and follow the Honorable Elijah Muhammad is the guiding goal of every Muslim. Mr. Muhammad teaches us the knowledge of our own selves, and of our own people. He cleans us up—morally, mentally and spiritually—and he reforms us of the vices that have blinded us here in the Western society. He stops black men from getting drunk, stops their dope addiction if they had it, stops nicotine, gambling, stealing, lying, cheating, fornication, adultery, prostitution, juvenile delinquency. I think of this whenever somebody talks about someone investigating us. Why investigate the Honorable Elijah Muhammad? They should subsidize him. He's cleaning up the mess that white men have made."

Malcolm's devotion to Elijah Muhammad was absolute. He never even considered the possibility that Elijah might have flaws. Malcolm believed that Elijah was divine, somewhat less than God, but greater than just a man.

Malcolm was crushed to discover that Elijah Muhammad was not perfect. In late 1962—a few months after the birth of Malcolm and Betty's third daughter, Ilyasah—Malcolm learned that Elijah Muhammad did not practice what he preached. It was strictly forbidden for men in the Nation of Islam to have sexual relations with women who were not their wives. Yet Elijah had fathered four children out of wedlock.

This news shook up everything Malcolm had believed in. He went to Elijah in early 1963 to ask if the stories were true. The leader admitted that they were, but said he hoped his weaknesses would be measured against his good deeds.

Malcolm did not feel sympathetic. He later wrote, "What began to break my faith was that, try as I might, I couldn't hide, I couldn't evade, that Mr. Muhammad, instead of facing what he had done before his followers, as a human weakness or as fulfillment of prophecy—which I sincerely believe that Muslims would have understood, or at least they would have accepted—Mr. Muhammad had, instead, been willing to hide, to cover up what he had done."

TENSION MOUNTS

By the early 1960s, the Nation of Islam had been infiltrated by spies. Whether these men were working for white people or for a black group that disagreed with the Nation of Islam's philosophies, Malcolm did not know. One thing was clear: the press was reporting on things that Malcolm had thought were happening in private. Someone at those meetings was leaking information to a white reporter.

After that, Malcolm could never be sure if what he was saying was truly private. He wasn't sure he could trust what he heard. False rumors kept cropping up.

Years later, information released through the Freedom of Information Act showed that New York police and FBI agents had paid men to join the Black Muslims and to report on what happened in meetings. It was becoming increasingly difficult for Malcolm to

President John F. Kennedy, fourth from the right, met with the leaders of the March on Washington in 1963.

keep a secret from the FBI. They always seemed to know where he was and what he was doing.

As tensions between Malcolm and Elijah grew, a national tragedy brought those tensions to a head. On Friday, November 22, 1963, President John F. Kennedy, the most popular U.S. president among African Americans since Franklin Delano Roosevelt, was assassinated in Dallas, Texas.

The death of the president was one of the saddest moments in U.S. history. The black community held its breath during the moments following the assassination, praying that a black man had not committed the crime. If a black man were accused of assassinating the president, people figured, racial violence would surely break out. When a white man was arrested for the crime, the black community relaxed.

Elijah Muhammad ordered his ministers to keep quiet about the death of the president. But keeping his mouth shut had never been Malcolm's style. On December 1, Malcolm had a speaking engagement at the Manhattan Center in New York City. During the question and answer period, he was asked to comment on President Kennedy's assassination. Defying Elijah Muhammad's orders, Malcolm said he thought it was a case of "the chickens coming home to roost."

Malcolm later claimed that he was discussing karma—that white people, by supporting or allowing violence against black people, were bound to bring violence upon themselves. But the press played the quote as if Malcolm was pleased that the president had been murdered.

Malcolm had not only involved the Nation of Islam in a controversy, but he had defied a direct order from Elijah Muhammad. As his punishment, Malcolm was ordered to stay silent in public for ninety days. Of his punishment, Malcolm said, "I felt as though something in *nature* had failed, like the sun, or the stars."

During his forced silence, Malcolm heard rumors leading him to believe that, once his punishment was over, all would not be forgotten. Word on the street was that Malcolm had betrayed and humiliated Elijah, and for this he would have to die.

By this time, everything Malcolm did made the news, whether he wanted the publicity or not. For example, reporters had written about his friendship with boxer Cassius Clay. The two men had become friends in 1962, after Clay and his brother attended a Nation of Islam meeting in Detroit.

On February 25, 1964, Clay fought Sonny Liston in Miami Beach, Florida, for the World Heavyweight Championship. Before the fight, Malcolm and Cassius prayed together. Malcolm told Cassius, "This fight is the *truth*. It's the Cross [a Christian symbol] and the Crescent [an Islamic symbol] fighting in a prize ring—for the first time. It's a modern Crusades—a Christian and a Muslim facing each other with television to beam it off Telstar [a communications satellite] for the whole world to see what happens! Do you

Malcolm X poses with world heavyweight boxing champion
Muhammad Ali as he signs autographs in New York City on
March 1, 1964.

think Allah has brought about all this intending for
you to leave the ring as anything but the champion?"

Clay went on to win boxing's greatest prize. Afterward,
he publically announced his membership in the Nation
of Islam and his new Islamic name—Muhammad Ali.

"MY NAME IS MUHAMMAD ALI"

On February 25, 1964, Cassius Clay defeated world heavyweight champion Sonny Liston in seven rounds, winning the World Heavyweight Championship. But right up until the moment the fight started, some insiders predicted it would never happen. Things were a mess. Two days before the fight, promoter Bill McDonald found out that Clay was a Black Muslim. McDonald threatened Clay, saying the fight would be canceled if he did not disavow the Nation of Islam. Clay refused. In the United States, everyone is guaranteed the freedom to choose and practice any religion.

The incident caused a public furor, and the Clay camp received many death threats. Before the fight, Malcolm X went to Clay's dressing room and they prayed together. Clay was paranoid because of the death threats. He declared that during the fight, only Muslims could give him drinking water and wipe his face. Even his longtime trainer, Angelo Dundee, was not allowed to touch Clay's face between rounds.

During the early rounds of the fight, Clay seemed content to frustrate and humiliate Liston. Bouncing on his toes, circling to Liston's left and leaning back to get out of range, Clay was an impossible target. Liston's punches missed so badly that they appeared clownish. When Clay did punch, it was with a quick left jab that was strong enough to pop Liston's head back.

Liston punched himself weary without getting close to Clay's chin. Clay saw Liston's panic and taunted him, calling the champion "old man."

According to the Liston camp, Sonny pulled a muscle in his shoulder while throwing a wild punch in the fourth round. An assistant rubbed ointment into the shoulder, and the ointment got into Clay's eyes in the fifth round. This made Clay lose his composure. He held Liston off, but he was stumbling and running. When the round ended, Clay screamed for Angelo Dundee to stop the fight.

"Have his gloves checked, have his gloves checked!" Clay shouted. Dundee knew the problem wasn't with Liston's gloves because they had never touched Clay's face. So the trainer did not ask for the fight to be stopped or the gloves checked. Instead, he supervised a one-minute washing of Clay's eyes and calmly told him that the problem was going to go away and he had to concentrate on winning the championship.

During the sixth round, Clay's vision gradually returned to normal. In the seventh round, Clay pounded Liston with combinations of punches. By the end of the round, Liston was through. Clay was awarded the victory when Liston failed to answer the bell to start the eighth round.

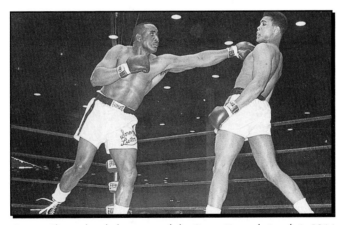

Cassius Clay, right, dodges a punch by Sonny Liston during their 1964 World Heavyweight Championship fight. After winning the fight, Clay announced his new name: Muhammad Ali.

Malcolm X gave a press conference on March 12, 1964, to publicize his split from the Nation of Islam.

Chapter **SIX**

TRUE ISLAM

IN MARCH 1964, MALCOLM CALLED A PRESS conference to announce that he was officially leaving the Nation of Islam. When he joined the organization, it had less than four hundred members. When he left, there were well over forty thousand.

The announcement of Malcolm's split from Elijah Muhammad made front-page news across the country. Members of the Nation of Islam viewed Malcolm's move as a betrayal. One Black Muslim who publicly criticized Malcolm for his break with the Nation of Islam was minister Louis Farrakhan. Farrakhan had been recruited into the Nation of Islam by Malcolm nine years earlier and had risen to a prominent position as leader of the group's Boston mosque.

A few days later, Malcolm announced that he was forming his own religious organization. It would be similar to the Nation of Islam—except its leader would not be worshiped. Malcolm never claimed to be a prophet.

The new organization was called the Muslim Mosque, Inc. At a press conference, Malcolm explained the purpose of the group: "This will give us a religious base, and the spiritual force necessary to rid our people of the vices that destroy the moral fiber of our community. Muslim Mosque, Inc. . . . will be the working base for an action program designed to eliminate the political oppression, the economic exploitation, and the social degradation suffered daily by twenty-two million Afro-Americans." He later wrote that he wanted to help "challenge the American black man to gain his human rights, and to cure his mental, spiritual, economic and political sicknesses."

Although many of Malcolm's beliefs changed when he left the Nation of Islam, his basic message remained the same. He still believed that blacks would achieve freedom only by fighting for it; that the U.S. government was racist and would not give rights to black people unless forced to do so; that patience was not a virtue for black citizens, who needed freedom now; that blacks who sided with whites in the social struggle should be hindered; and that blacks needed to choose their own leaders and take charge of their own social struggle.

Malcolm X and Martin Luther King Jr. met on March 26, 1964.

Although Malcolm sometimes supported boycotts and other forms of protest, for the most part he continued to dismiss the achievements of the Civil Rights movement. He had called Martin Luther King Jr.'s March on Washington the "Farce on Washington." "I don't believe we're going to overcome by singing," he said. "If you're going to get yourself a .45 and start singing 'We Shall Overcome,' I'm with you."

Malcolm was also not impressed when Congress passed the 1964 Civil Rights Act. He said that the new laws didn't go far enough—black people in northern ghettos were living a nightmare and would soon explode with rage. He cited outbreaks of racial violence

Malcolm X in the Semiramis Hotel in Cairo, Egypt, during his 1964 pilgrimage to Mecca.

in northern cities as evidence of the building anger. Malcolm's critics, white and black, continued to unjustly accuse him of promoting violence.

JOURNEY TO MECCA

Away from Elijah Muhammad's direction, Malcolm was free to think for himself. Perhaps recalling his father's work with Marcus Garvey, Malcolm began to think about the black struggle for independence in international terms. He also became more interested in exploring traditional Islam. Malcolm knew of the five demands required of traditional Muslims: 1) worship no one but Allah; 2) pray daily; 3) fast for one month of the year; 4) give to the poor; and 5) make a pilgrimage to Mecca, the Holy Land.

Malcolm decided that he should make what is called a *hajj,* a holy journey, or pilgrimage, to Mecca. Mecca is in Saudi Arabia. A journey there was not required of Black Muslims. The trip would have been far too expensive for most Black Muslims.

Malcolm told his sister Ella that he wanted to visit Mecca. But he didn't have enough money to finance the trip himself.

"How much do you need?" was all Ella asked.

Malcolm left on April 13, 1964, flying from John F. Kennedy Airport in New York City to his first stop in Frankfurt, Germany. His wife and children did not go with him. Malcolm spent a day in Frankfurt and was given a tour of the city. He was amazed at the friendliness of the German people.

From Frankfurt, Malcolm traveled to Cairo, Egypt. From there he joined a group of Muslim pilgrims (people making a journey for religious reasons) who were going to the city of Mecca. Malcolm felt strangely out of place among the traditional Muslims. He didn't know the prayers or the customs. He learned quickly, but at first he experienced something he had not expected. He felt like an outsider.

In Saudi Arabia, Malcolm's feelings about "the white man" began to change. He met light-skinned men—who would have been considered "white" in the United States—who were Muslims and who were his brothers in the faith.

In his travel journal, Malcolm wrote: "There were tens of thousands of pilgrims, from all over the world. They were of all colors, from blue-eyed blonds to black-skinned Africans. But we were all participating in the same ritual, displaying a spirit of unity and brotherhood that my experiences in America had led me to believe never could exist between the white and the non-white.

"America needs to understand Islam, because this is the one religion that erases from its society the race problem. . . .

"I could see from this, that perhaps if white Americans could accept the Oneness of God, then perhaps, too, they could accept *in reality* the Oneness of Man—and cease to measure, and hinder, and harm others in terms of their 'differences' in color."

Pilgrims on their way to Mecca were expected to wear the traditional covering of white cloths, one worn over the shoulder and the other around the waist. This was the way Malcolm dressed during his pilgrimage. He prayed and slept and ate next to Muslims of all colors.

In Mecca Malcolm prayed at the sacred stone in the Kaaba. The Kaaba is a place of worship originally used by Abraham and Ishmael four thousand years ago. The black stone inside the building is an important symbol of Islam.

While in the Holy Land, Malcolm wrote an open letter to the press in which he said: "[I am] spellbound by the graciousness I see displayed all around me by people of all colors. Despite my firm convictions, I have always been a man who tries to face facts, and to accept the reality of life as new experience and new knowledge unfolds it."

Following his stay in Mecca, Malcolm X again took a new name. He became el-Hajj Malik el-Shabazz. According to Islam, the Shabazz were a tribe of black people who migrated from East Asia to Africa fifty thousand years ago. *El-Hajj* meant that Malcolm had been to Mecca, and *Malik* is the Arabic version of his given name, Malcolm.

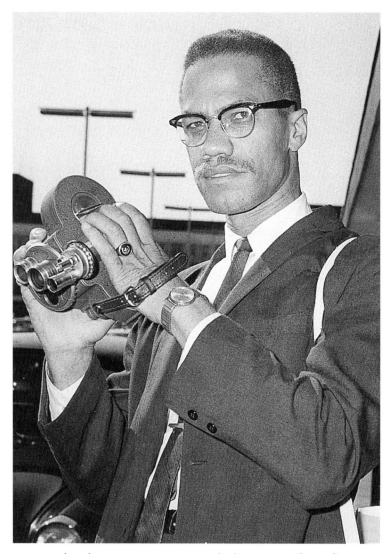

Equipped with a movie camera, Malcolm X waits for a flight at a London airport in July 1964.

Chapter **SEVEN**

WORLD LEADER

WHILE OVERSEAS, MALCOLM WAS GREETED BY leaders of other nations as though he were a world leader as well—which made the United States government very nervous. Here was a man who had the power to discuss foreign policy in international meetings, yet he had no official role in the U.S. government.

In April 1964, after his visit to Mecca, Malcolm received an audience with Prince Faisal, the ruler of Saudi Arabia. Faisal said he had heard of the Black Muslims, and from what he had read, they did not understand the true nature of Islam. Malcolm explained that he had separated from the Black Muslims and that his journey to Mecca was an attempt to understand Islam for the first time.

Saudi Arabian Prince Faisal, right, *and Malcolm X in 1964*

After next visiting Lebanon, Malcolm flew to Nigeria, where he was asked to speak at one of the nation's top colleges, Ibadan University. In his speech, he discussed his plans to link blacks in America with blacks from the rest of the world. Many activists of both races had called on black people to "return to Africa." But, Malcolm explained, this did not necessarily have to be done physically. It could be done economically.

Black Americans, with the help of African governments, could start their own businesses. Black consumers would buy only black-made products and trade only with black-owned businesses. In this way, black people would not have to depend on white people for anything. Malcolm believed that until blacks in the United States became economically independent, as many black Africans were, they would make little progress socially. This concept was called Pan-Africanism. It meant that all Africans would work together, even those who no longer lived in Africa.

Nigerian leaders told Malcolm that, according to the white Americans who did business in Nigeria, the American "Negro" was making much progress. Malcolm informed these leaders that the truth was less impressive.

From Nigeria, Malcolm flew to Accra, Ghana. There he saw white Americans who were in Africa to buy valuable underground minerals for cheap prices. Malcolm pointed out to the Ghanaians that the white men who wanted to rip off the Africans were smiling, but those men wouldn't think of smiling at a black face back in America.

During a press conference, Malcolm was corrected after he used the word *Negro*. A member of the Ghanaian press told Malcolm, "The word is not favored here, Mr. Malcolm X. The term Afro-American has greater meaning, and dignity."

Malcolm was given the opportunity to address the Ghanaian parliament, which functions much like the Congress in the United States. A state luncheon was also held in his honor by the Nigerian High Commissioner. At the luncheon, Malcolm was presented with a beautiful blue Nigerian dress robe to symbolize the fact that he was exactly like his African brothers. Malcolm also received a two-volume version of the Koran (the holy book of Islam) translated into English.

From Ghana, Malcolm traveled to Senegal, then on to Morocco, where he visited the famous Casbah. This Harlem-like community had formed when French troops occupying Morocco during World War II refused to allow dark-skinned Moroccans into certain parts of Casablanca, Morocco's largest city. Malcolm's last stop on his African tour was Algiers, Algeria, which was fighting for independence from the French.

Malcolm returned to New York on May 21, 1964, a changed man. He had gone to Africa to find his true religion. He learned that his earlier beliefs about race—that white people were devils and black people were the chosen ones—were false. He also learned that the rest of the world saw him as a representative of America's black population, which allowed him to achieve things he had never even dreamed of.

NEW DIRECTIONS

Back in New York, Malcolm returned to his family at their home in Queens, one of the city's five boroughs (sections). Malcolm's wife and daughters did not get to see him very often. Although he was a loving husband and father, he was among the world's busiest men. Betty spent much of her time answering the phone and taking messages for him. She took care of all family affairs. Malcolm admitted that he had never personally bought his daughters a present. Betty always took care of that for him. Even when Malcolm was in New York, he worked eighteen-hour days and came home only to sleep.

Technically, Malcolm's house in Queens belonged to the Nation of Islam. The organization had been threatening to kick him out of the house ever since he left the Nation of Islam. But he and his family were still living there. After Malcolm left the Nation, he supported his family with donations from the congregation of his mosque.

In June 1964, a few weeks after his thirty-ninth birthday, Malcolm formed another new organization. In addition to the Muslim Mosque, which was set up as a traditional Islamic temple, Malcolm wanted a nonreligious framework for his work. The new group, called the Organization of Afro-American Unity (OAAU), would "include all people of African descent in the Western Hemisphere, as well as our brothers and sisters on the African Continent." The OAAU would work for human rights for all black people, regardless of their differences.

Representing the OAAU, Malcolm returned to Africa and the Middle East for eighteen weeks in the summer and fall of 1964. Again he traveled without his family. During this trip, he met with many African leaders, including President Gamal Abdel Nasser of Egypt, President Nnamoi Azikiwe of

Nigeria, and President Julius Nyerere of Tanzania. By October, Malcolm had met with eleven heads of state in Africa.

There may have been an assassination attempt on Malcolm during his visit to Cairo, Egypt. He awoke in the middle of the night with severe stomach pain and had to have his stomach pumped. The diagnosis was food poisoning, but none of the people he ate with became ill. Since Malcolm had no known enemies in Africa, he suspected that someone had traveled far to harm him.

After this second trip to Africa, Malcolm stopped in New York briefly before traveling to France, where he

Malcolm holds his daughter Ilyasah at the John F. Kennedy airport in New York upon returning from his pilgrimage.

was scheduled to give a speech. Betty had recently given birth to their fourth daughter, Gamitah.

In New York, Malcolm told his followers: "My dearest friends have come to include *all* kinds—some Christians, Jews, Buddhists, Hindus, agnostics, and even atheists! I have friends who are called Capitalists, Socialists, and Communists! Some of my friends are moderates, conservatives, extremists—some are even Uncle Toms! My friends today are black, brown, red, yellow, and *white!*"

For years, white people who were sympathetic to Malcolm's ideas had been asking him what they could do to help. At one time, Malcolm had said there was nothing they could do, but now he changed his mind. He still did not allow white people to join his organization, but he did encourage them to teach other whites about social injustices in the United States.

Malcolm X faced many threats after his split with the Nation of Islam.

Chapter EIGHT

THREATS AND DANGER

MALCOLM HAD FELT FOR YEARS THAT HE WOULD die a violent death. He wrote, "If I take the kind of things in which I believe, then add to that the kind of temperament that I have, plus the one hundred percent dedication I have to whatever I believe in—these are ingredients which make it just about impossible for me to die of old age."

Malcolm also knew that he had enemies, both among white racists and in the Nation of Islam. Some Black Muslims had pledged to kill him for "betraying" Elijah Muhammad. And an incident in France convinced Malcolm that he had international enemies.

On February 9, 1965, he learned that his speaking engagement in France had been canceled. Declared an "undesirable person" by the French government, he was asked to leave the country. No official reason was given. But, according to some observers, French officials knew that someone might try to kill Malcolm, and they did not want to deal with the embarrassment and hassle of having him murdered in their country.

From France, Malcolm traveled to England, where he gave a series of interviews in the predominantly black area of Smethwick, near Birmingham. When the BBC, England's main broadcasting network, aired one of the interviews, Malcolm was criticized for stirring up racial tensions.

FIREBOMB

Malcolm returned to the United States on Saturday, February 13, 1965. The following day, at three o'clock in the morning, Malcolm, Betty, and their daughters were awakened by an explosion. Their house in Queens had been firebombed.

In a scene that must have reminded Malcolm of terrifying moments from his childhood, he screamed instructions in the dark as his house burned. He gathered up his children and made sure everyone got outside safely.

The bomb turned out to be a Molotov cocktail, a breakable container of gasoline with a rag fuse. Such a bomb is usually thrown through a window. When the container breaks, the fuse is triggered, causing a big explosion.

The New York City fire department needed a full hour to put out the fire. Half of Malcolm's home was destroyed. The family had no fire insurance. The threats on Malcolm's life were real—and his family was in danger as well. Malcolm took them to stay at a friend's house.

A few days later, Malcolm was invited by members of a civil rights group, the Student Nonviolent Coordinating Committee, to speak in Selma, Alabama. Members of Martin Luther King Jr.'s Southern Christian Leadership Conference tried to keep Malcolm from Selma, thinking that his presence would spark riots. Malcolm went anyway and spoke with his usual fervor. He saw the South as a good place to recruit new members to his mosque because of the growing frustration with the slow pace of progress through nonviolent protests.

STRUCK DOWN

Back in New York, Malcolm was scheduled to speak at the Audubon Ballroom in Harlem on Sunday afternoon, February 21, 1965. He invited Betty, who was again pregnant, and all four of his daughters to attend the meeting. With the house fire and the death threats, Malcolm had tried to keep his family clear of his activities, but on this day he asked them to watch him speak.

The Audubon Ballroom is on West 160th Street in Harlem, between Broadway and St. Nicholas Avenues, across the street from Columbia-Presbyterian Hospital. Four hundred wooden chairs had been set up in the ballroom. Security was surprisingly light. This was partially by Malcolm's design. He had forbidden high-security measures such as searching all guests at the door. He said that the frisking made everybody feel uncomfortable.

As was normal for Malcolm during such a meeting, he wore a dark suit, a white shirt, and a slender tie. He sat backstage listening to the preliminary speakers and planning his own remarks. Looking out at the room, he could see that three-quarters of the seats were full. On this day, he planned to talk not about the black man's battle against the white man, but rather about the foolishness of black men fighting other black men.

After the preliminary speeches, Malcolm was introduced. He moved to the front of the room and spoke his traditional greeting: "*Asalaikum* [Peace be with you], brothers and sisters."

Before he could begin his speech, however, a commotion broke out in the audience, and almost everyone, including Malcolm, looked out into the seats to see what was going on.

"Take your hand out of my pocket!" a man yelled.

Malcolm tried to calm the situation down. "Hold it! Hold it! Don't get excited," he said.

As this was going on, a smoke bomb was set off at the back of the auditorium. Someone poured water on

The aftermath of Malcolm X's assassination left chairs toppled in the Audubon Ballroom in Harlem, New York.

the bomb and put out the fire before the room could fill with smoke. A man sitting in the front row stood up, pulled a sawed-off shotgun from beneath his coat, and fired into Malcolm's chest. Two other men with handguns ran forward and pumped more bullets into Malcolm's body.

He was struck sixteen times by a combination of shotgun pellets and revolver bullets. Most of the shots hit his chest, but one struck his cheek and another hit the middle finger of his left hand. Malcolm's hand went to his chest when the firing started. Then his other arm flew up. As he fell over backward on the stage, his head hit the stagehand and he knocked over two chairs.

Chaos erupted in the auditorium. Betty ran onto the stage screaming. The shooters scattered in different directions. No two witnesses seemed to have seen the same thing.

One of the shooters, later identified as Talmadge Hayer, was chased from the ballroom by an armed member of Malcolm's security force. The security guard shot the assassin in the leg. Dragging his leg, Hayer made it to the sidewalk, but angry spectators began to kick him. The crowd might have killed him if police hadn't rescued him.

The police officers who were supposed to be stationed at the ballroom for Malcolm's appearance were nowhere to be seen. But two officers cruising by in a patrol car

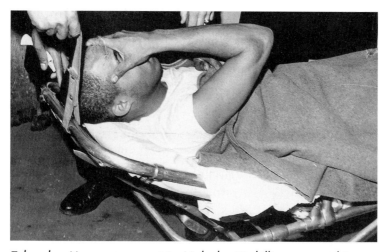

Talmadge Hayer, a suspect in Malcolm X's killing, covers his face as he is taken on a stretcher to Jewish Memorial Hospital.

had seen the angry mob kicking the assailant. The police fired two warning shots into the air to break up the attack.

Someone ran across the street to Columbia-Presbyterian Hospital and grabbed a stretcher. Malcolm was taken to the hospital, where he was pronounced dead on the operating table at 3:15 P.M.

The next day, Elijah Muhammad commented on Malcolm's death. His words were reminiscent of Malcolm's "chickens coming home to roost" statement following the assassination of President Kennedy. Muhammad said, "Malcolm died according to his preaching. He seems to have taken weapons as his god. Therefore, we couldn't tolerate a man like that. He preached war. We preach peace."

That same day, the Black Muslim Mosque Number Seven in Harlem was firebombed. The bomb caused a five-alarm fire. During the fire, a wall collapsed and two fire engines parked at the curb were smashed. Five firefighters were injured battling the blaze.

Because of the potential for violence, it was difficult for Betty to find a location for Malcolm's funeral. Bishop Alvin Childs agreed to hold the funeral at Harlem's Faith Temple, a former movie theater that could hold fourteen hundred people.

When people in Harlem learned that Malcolm had died without any money, leaving Sister Betty and the girls with no savings, no insurance, and no income, a fund was set up to help the family get by.

Norman 3X Butler, left, and Thomas 15X Johnson, right, at the police station after their arrests

Within two weeks of the assassination, two more men were arrested for the shooting. They were Norman 3X Butler and Thomas 15X Johnson, both members of the Nation of Islam.

MOURNING MALCOLM

After his death, Malcolm's body was displayed for public viewing in a glass-covered coffin at the Unity Funeral Home in Harlem. Twenty-two thousand people came to see him.

After the viewing, Malcolm's body was prepared for burial according to Muslim traditions. Sheik Ahmed Hassoun, Malcolm's spiritual adviser and a teacher at the Muslim Mosque, Inc., performed the ritual. He

bathed the body in holy oils and draped it in seven
white linen shrouds so that only his face could be seen.

As big as the Faith Temple was, it was nowhere near
large enough for the throng that wanted to attend
Malcolm's funeral. Besides the seventeen hundred
mourners packed into the building, more than six
thousand people lined the streets outside.

*Members of the press pay their respects to Malcolm X at the
Unity Funeral Home. The glass that covered Malcolm's open
coffin during public viewing was removed for press photos.*

Young Betty, pregnant with twins, mourns at the grave of Malcolm X at the Ferncliff Cemetery in Hartsdale, New York. More than seventeen hundred people paid their respects at his funeral on February 27, 1965.

Actor Ossie Davis delivered Malcolm's eulogy. He said, "Many will ask what Harlem finds to honor in this stormy, controversial and bold young captain—and we will smile. . . . They will say that he is of hate—a fanatic, a racist—who can only bring evil to the cause for which you struggle."

"And we will answer and say unto them: Did you ever talk to Brother Malcolm? Did you ever touch him, or have him smile at you? Did you ever really listen to him? Did he ever do a mean thing? Was he ever himself associated with violence or any public disturbance? For if you did you would know him. And if you knew him you would know why we must honor him: Malcolm was our manhood, our living, black manhood! This was his meaning to his people. And, in honoring him, we honor the best in ourselves."

UNANSWERED QUESTIONS

There are several reasons to doubt that the New York police fully solved the crime of Malcolm's assassination. Initial reports indicated that at least five men were involved in the shooting—three who fired weapons and two who created the diversion in the auditorium. But once the police had arrested the three shooters, they stopped looking for other assailants.

Hayer, from the time he first confessed to shooting Malcolm, insisted that Johnson and Butler had nothing to do with the assassination. It is puzzling that Malcolm's security guards did not notice Johnson and Butler entering the ballroom, since they were followers of Elijah Muhammad. Hayer was not a Muslim, and he said that the Black Muslims did not pay him to murder Malcolm. He did admit that he had committed the crime for money, but he never identified who had paid him—or who his accomplices were.

Whoever was responsible for the crime, Malcolm always knew that he had enemies and that his life was in danger. In the last chapter of his autobiography, he wrote: "I know that societies often have killed the people who have helped to change those societies. And if I can die having brought any light, having exposed any meaningful truth that will help to destroy the racist cancer that is malignant in the body of America—then, all of the credit is due to Allah."

LOUIS FARRAKHAN

By the time of Malcolm's death, the Nation of Islam had spread to more than sixty cities in the United States and to Ghana, Mexico, and Caribbean countries. In 1972 Elijah appointed Louis Farrakhan as the new spokesman for the Nation. Farrakhan was born Louis Eugene Walcott on May 11, 1933, in Roxbury, Massachusetts, and was raised by his mother, a native of St. Kitts, an island in the Caribbean Sea. His mother taught him about the African American struggle for equality, freedom, and justice.

Recognizing Louis's musical talent, his mother gave him a violin for his sixth birthday. A child prodigy, by age thirteen he had played with the Boston College Orchestra and the Boston Civic Symphony. The following year, he became famous coast to coast when he won a talent contest on the *Ted Mack Amateur Hour,* a popular TV show of the time. As an entertainer, he became known as "The Charmer."

Louis graduated from high school at age sixteen. Because he'd also been a track and field star, he earned a scholarship to Winston-Salem Teachers' College in North Carolina, where he excelled in English.

Louis married his childhood sweetheart in September 1953, during his senior year. Needing money to support his new family, he quit college and became a professional performing artist—singing, dancing, and playing the violin. In February 1955, while appearing in a show called *Calypso Follies,* Louis was invited by Malcolm X to visit the Nation of Islam's Temple Number Two. Soon afterward, Louis joined the organization and became known as Louis X.

He gave up show business and became a minister for the Nation of Islam's Boston temple in 1956. At first Louis was a devoted follower of Malcolm, even patterning his speaking style after Malcolm's. But when Malcolm split from the Nation of Islam, Louis turned on him, calling him a traitor. (Malcolm's family feels Farrakhan turned on Malcolm earlier than he admits.) After Malcolm X was assassinated, Louis became the head of the Nation's Harlem mosque. He quickly became the Nation's number one spokesman, continuing to promote Elijah Muhammad's teachings even after Elijah died.

Farrakhan has been the spokesman for the Nation for almost thirty years. Under his leadership, the Black Muslims have thrived. In 1995 Farrakhan organized the successful Million Man March in Washington, D.C. Hundreds of thousands of black men attended the march and vowed to renew their commitment to family, community, and personal responsibility.

While the Nation of Islam works to create healthier black individuals and communities, it has been heavily criticized for its hateful teachings about white people, especially Jewish people. Many black leaders, such as the Reverend Jesse Jackson, have condemned Farrakhan's anti-Semitic remarks.

The Nation still talks of Martians being involved in the creation of the world. In 1995 Farrakhan told a gathering that he had had a vision of a UFO. He said that Martians had abducted him and taken him to the mother ship, where he met Elijah Muhammad, who gave Louis the idea for the Million Man March.

Unlike Malcolm X, who never had any money of his own, Louis Farrakhan lives in luxury in a mansion in Michigan. He is the father of nine children and has many grandchildren and great-grandchildren. He still maintains a grueling work schedule.

This rare photo of a smiling Malcolm X was taken in London in July 1964.

Chapter **NINE**

MALCOLM'S LEGACY

MALCOLM X'S AUTOBIOGRAPHY WAS PUBLISHED not long after his death. It was the book he had written with journalist Alex Haley. The two first worked together when Haley interviewed Malcolm for an adult magazine. They collaborated on the autobiography for two years. Malcolm was suspicious of Haley at first but eventually came to trust the non-Muslim author. *Time* magazine called *The Autobiography of Malcolm X* one of the ten most important nonfiction books of the twentieth century.

Malcolm's message of black pride and self-sufficiency helped inspire more radical political movements that took off after his death, such as the "black power" movement and the Black Panther Party. Black power activists believed, as Malcolm did, that black people should not try to fit in with white society, but rather should create a social and economic system for themselves. The black power movement considered Malcolm its hero. The Black Panther Party, organized in 1966, advocated full employment and decent housing for black people; an end to police brutality; and the teaching of black history. Black Panther members, wearing black leather jackets and black berets and carrying guns, patrolled the streets of black neighborhoods.

After Malcolm's death, Betty gave birth to twin girls, Malikah and Malaak, whom she'd been carrying when her husband was shot. She raised the girls in the suburb of Mount Vernon, just north of New York City. In 1975 Betty earned her doctorate degree in education at the University of Massachusetts. She became the director of public relations at Medgar Evans College in Brooklyn and later the head of the school's Office of Institutional Advancement.

In 1990 a Manhattan court clerk named Doug Henderson, who was reportedly obsessed with Malcolm X, broke into a safe and stole the blood-stained diary that Malcolm had in his suit jacket at the time of his death. Henderson got caught when he tried to sell the diary for five thousand dollars. He was arrested and eventually sentenced to five years on probation. After his sentencing, the diary was given to Malcolm's daughters.

Betty Shabazz, pictured here in the late 1980s, received her doctorate degree in 1975.

MEMORIES AND ENDINGS

After Malcolm's death, Betty Shabazz publicly accused Nation of Islam leader Louis Farrakhan of having a role in the assassination. Two months before Malcolm's murder, Farrakhan had written that Malcolm was a "traitor" and that "such a man is worthy of death." Almost twenty years later, the feud made headlines again. In 1994 Malcolm and Betty's daughter Qubilah was arrested and charged with

Qubilah leaves the Federal Court Building in Minneapolis, Minnesota, after her initial hearing regarding accusations that she hired a hit man to assassinate Louis Farrakhan.

plotting to hire a hit man to kill Farrakhan. Those charges were dropped for lack of evidence.

On June 1, 1997, Betty was badly burned in a fire at her apartment in the New York City borough of Yonkers. The fire was set by her twelve-year-old grandson, who was named after Malcolm X. Betty had been caring for the boy, who wanted to return to his mother, Qubilah, in Texas.

Betty was visited in the hospital by many dignitaries, including the Reverend Jesse Jackson, poet Maya Angelou, Martin Luther King Jr.'s widow, Coretta Scott King, political activist Dick Gregory, and former New York City mayor David Dinkins. Over the next three weeks, Betty underwent five operations to replace her burned tissues with artificial skin. But people with such severe burn injuries rarely survive, and Betty passed away on June 23. She was buried atop Malcolm at the Ferncliff Cemetery in Hartsdale, New York.

In 1985, after serving nineteen years in prison, convicted assassin Norman 3X Butler (by then known as Muhammad Abdul Aziz) was released on parole. In March 1998, Aziz was appointed by the Nation of Islam to head the same Harlem mosque (Number Seven) where Malcolm X had preached during the 1950s. Aziz still proclaims his innocence in Malcolm's death. The Nation of Islam hired a lie detector expert to interview Aziz about the assassination. After three

Former NAACP head Benjamin F. Muhammad, right, introduces Muhammad Abdul Aziz, center, as the new head of the Nation of Islam's Harlem temple.

days of questioning, the expert proclaimed that Aziz was telling the truth when he said he had nothing to do with Malcolm X's death.

Looking for Answers

In April 2000, Malcolm's daughter Attallah Shabazz met face to face with Louis Farrakhan—the first-ever meeting between him and a member of Malcolm's family. Attallah was just six years old when she saw her father murdered. Her conversation with Farrakhan was videotaped by the TV show *60 Minutes* and televised the following month on CBS.

Although Farrakhan denied that he had directly ordered Malcolm's assassination, he did admit to saying things that might have been taken to mean it was alright to kill Malcolm. He accepted partial blame for the killing.

Farrakhan explained: "As I may have been complicit in words that I spoke. . . . I acknowledge that and regret that any word that I have said caused the loss of life of a human being."

Farrakhan had previously claimed that the FBI played a part in Malcolm's death. "This is bigger than the Nation of Islam," Farrakhan said.

"You can't keep pointing fingers," Attallah said during their talk. "My father was not killed from a grassy knoll," she added, referring to the mystery that still surrounds the assassination of President John F. Kennedy.

Mike Wallace, with his back to the camera, *interviews Louis Farrakhan and Attallah Shabazz for the May 14, 2000, edition of 60 Minutes.*

Farrakhan replied, "Yes, it is true that black men pulled the trigger. We cannot deny any responsibility in this. Where we are responsible, where our hands are a part of this, we beg God's mercy and forgiveness."

A MODERN HERO

Malcolm X has not been forgotten. He remains a cultural hero for black people and for anyone who believes in racial justice and ethnic pride. Many books have been written about Malcolm's life and message.

Several cities in America, including Savannah, Georgia, have annual Malcolm X festivals in May to celebrate Malcolm's birthday. In 1992 filmmaker Spike Lee made a major motion picture about Malcolm X, starring Denzel Washington in the title role. The movie helped rekindle Malcolm's message. T-shirts, posters, and baseball caps bear Malcolm's image or the symbol "X." He is praised in the lyrics of rap songs, and his speeches are available on CD. Malcolm

Denzel Washington played the lead in Spike Lee's 1992 film Malcolm X.

is an icon for young people, even those who do not entirely understand his message.

On May 19, 2000, which would have been Malcolm's seventy-fifth birthday, more than seven hundred admirers gathered in the pouring rain at his graveside in Westchester County, New York. One of the visitors was Jean Reynolds, who was in the Audubon Ballroom when Malcolm X was assassinated. "This is a true blessing regardless of the weather," Reynolds said.

Michael X, a Bronx community activist, added, "I'm glad we didn't bury Malcolm's legacy along with him. And all these people coming here today shows how much he truly means to our community. His clarity of thought, integrity, vision, courage and, most of all, his humility separated him from the pack when he was alive and even more so today."

SOURCES

13   Steven F. Lawson, *Running for Freedom: Civil Rights and Black Politics in America Since 1941* (Philadelphia: Temple University Press, 1991), 6.

14   Malcolm X, with Alex Haley, *The Autobiography of Malcolm X* (New York: Ballantine Books, 1964), 11.

14   Ibid., 6.

17   Ibid., 37–38.

17   Ibid., 41–42.

20   Walter Dean Myers, *Malcolm X: By Any Means Necessary* (New York: Scholastic Press, 1993), 43.

22   Malcolm X, with Alex Haley, 61.

22   *Malcolm X: A Search for Identity*, A&E Biography, Newvideo, 1995, videocassette.

22   Malcolm X, with Alex Haley, 67.

24   *Malcolm X: A Search for Identity.*

25   Jack Rummel, *Malcolm X: Militant Black Leader* (Los Angeles, Melrose Square, 1988), 39.

30   *Malcolm X: A Search for Identity*

30   Ibid.

38   Alex Haley, "The Playboy Interview with Malcolm X," *Playboy,* May 1963.

48   "Malcolm X," *Microsoft Encarta Online Encyclopedia 2001*, 1997, Microsoft Corp. <http://encarta.msn.htm> (May 18, 2001).

48   Imam Benjamin Karin, ed., *The End of White World Supremacy: Four Speeches by Malcolm X* (New York: Merit, 1965), 48.

53   George Breitman, Herman Porter, and Baxter Smith, *The Assassination of Malcolm X* (New York: Pathfinder Press, 1991), 22.

53   *Malcolm X: A Search for Identity.*

54   Breitman, 38.

56   Haley.

56   Ibid.

57   Ibid.

58 Ibid.
59 Malcolm X, with Alex Haley, 312.
61 Ibid., 329.
62 Ibid., 333.
63 Ibid., 335.
68 Ibid., 346.
68 Ibid., 345.
69 Myers, 130.
71 Malcolm X, with Alex Haley, 347.
72 Ibid., 371–72.
73 Rummel, 165.
77 Malcolm X, with Alex Haley, 386.
79 Myers, 158.
81 Malcolm X, with Alex Haley, 410.
83 Ibid., 414.
86 Rummel, 175.
86 Malcolm X, with Alex Haley, 473.
86 David Shirley, *Malcolm X: Minister of Justice*,
    (Philadelphia: Chelsea House Publishers, 1994), 28.
89 Malcolm X, with Alex Haley, 479.
92 Ibid., 494.
93 Ibid., 417–18.
99 "Farrakhan: I had Malcolm X slay role," *The Daily
    News,* May 11, 2000, 40.
102 William Neuman, "Malcolm X's daughter talks with
    Farrakhan," *The New York Post,* May 9, 2000, 40.
102 "Farrakhan: I had Malcolm X slay role."
102 Ibid.
103 Ibid.
105 Jack Baxter, "Followers flock to Malcolm X's grave on
    his 75th birthday," *New York Post,* May 20, 2000, 18.
105 Ibid.

SELECTED BIBLIOGRAPHY

BOOKS

Breitman, George, Herman Porter, and Baxter Smith. *The Assassination of Malcolm X*. New York: Pathfinder Press, 1991.

Goldman, Peter. *The Death and Life of Malcolm X*. New York: Harper & Row, 1973.

Halasa, Malu. *Elijah Muhammad: Religious Leader*. New York: Chelsea House, 1990.

Malcolm X, with Alex Haley. *The Autobiography of Malcolm X*. New York: Ballantine Books, 1964.

Myers, Walter Dean. *Malcolm X: By Any Means Necessary*. New York: Scholastic Press, 1993.

Patterson, Charles. *The Civil Rights Movement*. New York: Facts on File, 1995.

Rummel, Jack. *Malcolm X: Militant Black Leader*. Los Angeles: Melrose Square, 1988.

Shirley, David. *Malcolm X: Minister of Justice*. Philadelphia: Chelsea House Publishers, 1994.

PERIODICALS

Baxter, Jack. "Followers flock to Malcolm X's grave on his 75th birthday." *New York Post*, May 20, 2000,.

"Farrakhan: I had Malcolm X slay role." *The Daily News*, May 11, 2000.

Italiano, Laura. "Clerk admits stealing diary in Malcolm X murder case." *New York Post*, July 14, 2000.

Neuman, William. "Malcolm X's daughter talks with Farrakhan." *New York Post*, May 9, 2000.

Ross, Barbara. "Guilty plea in theft of Malcolm X diary." *The Daily News*, July 18, 2000.

VIDEOS

Malcolm X: A Search for Identity. A&E Biography. Newvideo, 1995.

INDEX

African Communities League, 9
Ali, Muhammad. *See* Clay,
   Cassius
Audubon Ballroom, 85–87, 105
*Autobiography of Malcolm X,
   The*, 97
Aziz, Muhammad Abdul, 101

Black Muslims, 30–32, 34, 43,
   45, 52, 58, 60, 67, 71, 75,
   83, 93, 95
Black Panther Party, 97–98
Butler, Norman 3X, 90, 93, 101

Civil Rights Act (1964), 69–70
Civil Rights movement, 13,
   45–48, 56, 69
Clay, Cassius (Muhammad
   Ali), 62–65
Congress of Racial Equality
   (CORE), 13

Faisal, Prince of Saudi
   Arabia, 75–76
Farrakhan, Louis, 67, 94–95,
   99–100, 102-103
Federal Bureau of
   Investigation (FBI), 53–54,
   60–61

Garvey, Marcus, 8–9, 42

el-Hajj Malik el-Shabazz, 39,
   73
Haley, Alex, 57–58, 97

Harlem, 23-27, 41–45, 85–87,
   89–91
Hayer, Talmadge, 88, 93
Hinton, Johnson, 43–45

Ibadan University, 76
Islam, 71–73, 75

Jarvis, Shorty, 19–22, 24, 27, 29
Johnson, Thomas 15X, 90, 93

King Jr., Martin Luther,
   46–47, 69
Ku Klux Klan (KKK), 11–12

Lee, Spike, 104
Little, Earl (father), 8-9,
   14–15, 42
Little, Earl (brother), 9
Little, Ella (half sister), 9,
   16–17, 41–42, 71
Little, Hilda (sister), 8
Little, Louise (mother), 8–9,
   15–16
Little, Malcolm. *See* Malcolm X
Little, Mary (half sister), 9
Little, Philbert (brother), 8,
   30, 33
Little, Reginald (brother), 8,
   30, 33
Little, Robert (brother), 8
Little, Wesley (brother), 8
Little, Wilfred (brother), 8,
   37–38
Little, Yvonne (sister), 8

Lomax, Louis, 51

Malcolm X: assassination,
85–92; birth and childhood,
8–17; Black Muslims, 30–32,
34–35; in Boston, 18–23,
29–30; in Harlem, 24–27;
investigated by FBI, 52–55,
59–61; journey to Mecca,
70–73; legacy, 97–105;
marriage to Betty Sanders,
42–43; Nation of Islam,
30–32, 34–35, 38–42, 43–45,
94–95; prison, 30–35, 37;
split from Nation of Islam,
58–59, 61–62, 67; threats
against him, 83–85; views
contrasting with Civil
Rights movement, 45–49,
69–70
Malcolm X (film), 104
Mecca, 71–73, 75
The Mike Wallace Show, 51
Muhammad, Elijah (Elijah
Poole), 30–32, 34–35, 38–42,
48, 51–53, 54–56, 58–59,
61–62, 67, 70, 83, 89, 93,
94–95
Muhammad Speaks, 48–49
Muhammad, Wallace D., 55–56
Muslim Mosque, Inc., 68, 79,
90

National Association for the
Advancement of Colored
People (NAACP), 13
Nation of Islam, 30–33,
38–40, 42, 45, 47–49, 51–56,
59, 62–63, 66–68, 79, 83,

94–95, 99, 101–102
Norfolk Prison Colony, 32

Organization of Afro-
American Unity (OAAU), 79

Parks, Rosa, 45–46

Roseland Ballroom, 20, 22

Saudi Arabia, 71–73, 75
segregation, 6-8, 10–12, 13
Shabazz, Attallah X
(daughter), 43, 102–103
Shabazz, Betty X (wife), 42,
43, 54, 58, 78–80, 85, 88–89,
98
Shabazz, Gamitah X
(daughter), 80
Shabazz, Ilyasah X
(daughter), 58, 74
Shabazz, Malaak X
(daughter), 98
Shabazz, Malikah X
(daughter), 98
Shabazz, Qubilah X
(daughter), 54, 99–100
60 Minutes, 102
Small's Paradise, 24–25
Southern Christian
Leadership Conference,
47–48, 85
Student Nonviolent
Coordinating Committee, 85

Universal Negro Improvement
Association (UNIA), 9, 11–12

Wallace, Mike, 51, 103

OTHER TITLES FROM LERNER AND A&E®:

Arthur Ashe
The Beatles
Benjamin Franklin
Bill Gates
Bruce Lee
Carl Sagan
Chief Crazy Horse
Christopher Reeve
Edgar Allan Poe
Eleanor Roosevelt
George W. Bush
George Lucas
Gloria Estefan
Jack London
Jacques Cousteau
Jane Austen
Jesse Owens
Jesse Ventura
Jimi Hendrix
John Glenn
Latin Sensations

Legends of Dracula
Legends of Santa Claus
Louisa May Alcott
Madeleine Albright
Mark Twain
Maya Angelou
Mohandas Gandhi
Mother Teresa
Nelson Mandela
Oprah Winfrey
Princess Diana
Queen Cleopatra
Queen Latifah
Rosie O'Donnell
Saint Joan of Arc
Thurgood Marshall
William Shakespeare
Wilma Rudolph
Women in Space
Women of the Wild West

ABOUT THE AUTHOR

Michael Benson, originally from Rochester, New York, received his bachelor's degree in Communication Arts from Hofstra University. He is the author of fifteen books, including the BIOGRAPHY® title *Gloria Estefan.* He currently works as a magazine editor and lives in Brooklyn, New York, with his wife, daughter, and son.

PHOTO ACKNOWLEDGMENTS

Photographs used with the permission of: AP/Wide World Photos, pp. 2, 27, 49, 52, 63, 66, 87, 90 (both), 91, 100, 101, 103; Corbis/Bettmann, pp. 6, 9, 10, 28, 31, 40, 46, 55, 57, 69, 80, 82; National Archives (306-NT-650-1), p. 12; Schomburg Center for Research in Black Culture, pp. 18, 21, 43; Pittsburgh Courier Archives/Archive Photos, p. 33; Archive Photos, pp. 36, 50, 76; Mallory Photo/Schomburg Center for Research in Black Culture, p. 44; John F. Kennedy Library, p. 60; Deutsche Presse Agentur/ Archive Photos, p. 65; Express Newspapers/Archive Photos, pp. 70, 74, 96; Corbis/Bettmann-UPI, pp. 88, 92; Bjorg/Archive Photos, p. 99; Photofest, p.104.

Front and Back Covers: Schomburg Center for Research in Black Culture